Also available:

Mima's Choices

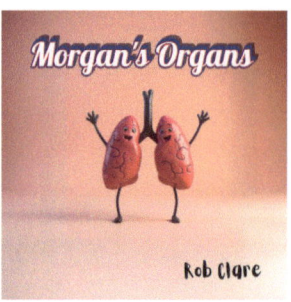
Morgan's Organs

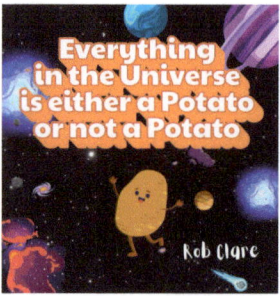
Everything in the Universe is Either a Potato or not a Potato

Don't Shake This Book

A to Z of Feelings and Emotions

Hello, Goodbye
www.robclarebooks.com

Copyright © 2025 Rob Clare Books
All rights reserved. No part of this book may be used or reproduced by any means, graphic, electronic, or mechanical, including photocopying, recording, taping or by any information storage retrieval system without the written permission of the author except in the case of brief quotations embodied in critical articles and reviews.
First originally published by Rob Clare Books 2025

Hello and Goodbye Around the World

Scan the QR Code and you'll be able to listen to how 'Hello, Good Morning' and 'Goodbye, Goodnight' is spoken in each different language

*In some of the languages, diacritics are used—these are the special characters found in the alphabets of those countries. Pronounciations of spoken words are provided in blue at the bottom of each page.

United Kingdom
We speak English

"Hello, good morning!" says Olivia as we arrive in London, the capital of England, in the United Kingdom.

We ride a red double-decker bus past Big Ben and the Tower of London. Then we hop on an underground train, called the Tube, and visit Buckingham Palace to see the royal family. The guards outside all wear tall, funny hats. We finish our tour with a cozy stop at a café for a cup of tea and some warm scones.

Hello, good morning ⟶ heh-loh, good mor-ning

We visit the other countries of the United Kingdom. In Scotland, we hike the Highlands, explore castles, and search for the Loch Ness Monster. In Wales, we marvel at the green hills and tall mountains. In Northern Ireland, we stand in awe at the Giant's Causeway.

We finish our journey back in England, stopping at Stonehenge to watch the sunset. We enjoy a tasty dinner of fish and chips, with warm apple crumble for dessert. Archie waves. **"Goodbye, goodnight!"** he says.

Goodbye, good night → good-bye, good nite

Germany

Wir sprechen Deutsch
We speak German

"Hallo, guten Morgen!" says Anna as we arrive in Germany at the beautiful medieval town of Schiltach, tucked in the heart of the Black Forest. The half-timbered houses and cobblestone streets make it feel like we've stepped back in time.

We snack on warm, salty pretzels from a local bakery and watch the treetops of the forest gently sway in the morning breeze. Later, we visit Neuschwanstein Castle, the towering fairy-tale castle that inspired Sleeping Beauty, and imagine knights, kings, and princesses.

Hallo, guten Morgen → hah-loh, goo-ten mor-gen

We sail along the Rhine River, enjoying the vineyards, castles, and small towns we see along the way. We arrive in Berlin, the capital of Germany, and explore the famous Brandenburg Gate, the Berlin Wall, and the Fernsehturm tower.

We stop for a hearty dinner of bratwurst, crispy schnitzel, and warm spaetzle. As the stars begin to twinkle above Berlin, we leave the city's excitement behind for our next adventure.

"Tschüss, gute Nacht!" says Lukas.

Tschüss, gute Nacht → chooss, goo-teh nahkt

Italy

Noi parliamo italiano
We speak Italian

"Ciao, buongiorno!" says Maria as we arrive in Rome, the sun warming the ancient streets of Italy's bustling capital. We enjoy creamy, colourful gelato as we wander past the famous Colosseum, toss a coin into the sparkling Trevi Fountain, and climb the grand Spanish Steps.

There are so many beautiful places in Italy that we could spend days exploring and still not see them all!

Ciao, buongiorno

Ciao, buongiorno → chow, bwon-jor-noh

We travel to other amazing places in Italy, marvelling at the Leaning Tower of Pisa as it tilts skyward, admiring the grand Duomo in Florence with its colourful dome, and gliding through the canals of Venice in a gondola.

For dinner, we enjoy a delicious feast of pizza and creamy spaghetti carbonara, the warm aromas filling the air. Now it's time to leave Italy and continue our adventure. Antonio waves and smiles. **"Arrivederci, buonanotte,"** he says.

Arrivederci, buonanotte → ah-ree-veh-der-chee, bwo-nah-not-teh

France

Nous parlons français
We speak French

"**Bonjour!**" says Pierre as we explore the wonders of France. We see the castles of the Loire Valley. In Provence, the lavender fields stretch out like purple oceans. Along the sunny beaches of Nice, the sparkling blue waves tickle our toes.
For breakfast, we pause at a cozy café to enjoy warm, flaky croissants and sip aromatic coffee, the buttery smell making our mouths water.

Bonjour → bon-zhoor

We arrive in Paris, the capital of France. We climb to the top of the Eiffel Tower, visit Notre-Dame Cathedral, and see the sparkling glass pyramid at the Louvre, where we find the famous Mona Lisa painting.

We stop for a delicious dinner of baguettes, cheese, and crêpes with strawberries.
We leave France ready for our next adventure.
"Au revoir, bonne nuit," says Éloïse.

Au revoir, bonne nuit → oh ruh-vwar, bun nwee

Netherlands

We spreken Nederlands

We speak Dutch

"Hallo, goedemorgen!" says Lars as we arrive in Amsterdam, the capital of the Netherlands. We ride bikes along the canals and see houses with steep roofs and big windows. We wave at boats as they drift under little bridges. We stop for some delicious stroopwafels and dutch pancakes.

Hallo, goedemorgen → hah-loh, khoo-duh-mor-ghen

We travel to the Keukenhof Gardens, filled with rows and rows of flowers called tulips. We go to the countryside, where we see windmills and traditional farmhouses, and shops that sell wooden shoes called clogs.

Dinner is pea soup called erwtensoep, with crispy croquettes, cheese we picked up at the bustling markets, and sweet apple pie with whipped cream.
As the sky glows orange with the setting sun, it's time to leave the Netherlands behind. Mila waves and smiles. **"Dag, goedenacht,"** she says.

Dag, goedenacht → dahkh, hoo-duh-nahkt

Sweden
Vi talar svenska
We speak Swedish

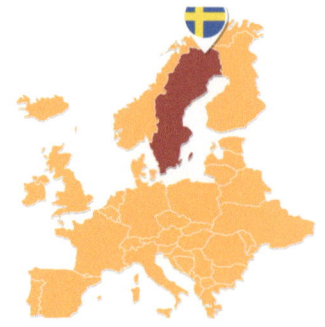

"Hej, god morgon!" says Freja as we arrive in Stockholm, the sparkling capital of Sweden. We explore a grand palace with gleaming golden rooms, then wander through a fascinating Viking ship museum, imagining the brave sailors of long ago.

We venture into the countryside, with fields of blooming wildflowers and charming red wooden houses scattered among the many shimmering lakes.

Birds sing from the treetops, and the fresh, crisp air fills our lungs as we explore this peaceful, beautiful land.

Hej, god morgon → hey, good mor-ron

We snack on warm cinnamon buns and travel north through snowy forests to visit the traditional Sami people, who herd reindeer and make birchwood carvings.

Dinner is meatballs with lingonberry jam and mashed potatoes. As the snow gently falls over the forest and the Northern Lights glow in the sky, Anita says, **"Hej då, god natt."**

Hej då, god natt → hey doh, good naht

Turkey

Biz Türkçe konuşuyoruz

We speak Turkish

"**Merhaba, günaydın!**" says Yasmin as we arrive in Istanbul, a magical city in Turkey. We hear the call to prayer from tall minarets, visit the Blue Mosque, eat Turkish delight, and sip tea beside the Bosphorus River, where Europe and Asia meet.

Merhaba günaydın!

Merhaba, günaydın → mehr-hah-bah, goo-nah-ee-duhn

We explore the huge Grand Bazaar market, looking at handmade rugs and textiles. We travel to the fairy chimneys of Cappadocia, swim in warm waters, marvel at the terraces at Pamukkale, and explore ancient ruins.

Dinner is kebabs, lentil soup, and sweet baklava with honey and nuts.

As the moon rises, Emir smiles. He waves at us as we travel on to our next destination. **"Hoşçakal, iyi geceler,"** he says.

Hoşça kal, iyi geceler → hosh-cha kahl, ee-yee geh-jeh-ler

Russia

My govorím pa-rússki
(Мы говорим по-русски)
We speak Russian

"Privet, dobroye utro!" says Alexei as we arrive in Moscow, the capital of Russia. We visit Red Square and look up at the colourful onion domes of St. Basil's Cathedral. We stroll through Gorky Park, and ride a fast metro train with chandeliers!

It's very cold and snow is falling. We stop for some pelmeni dumplings and buy some Matryoshka dolls for souvenirs.

Privet, dobroye utro (Привет, доброе утро)
→ **pree-vyet, doh-bro-yeh oot-rah**

We see snowy forests, visit the city of Saint Petersburg, and wander through the Hermitage Museum. We slip and slide as we ice skate at Moskovsky Victory Park. In the evening, we're excited to watch a ballet performance, where the ballerinas spin and twirl.

For dinner we try warm borscht soup and sweet blinis with jam. The rich smells fill the restaurant as the snow falls outside. Wrapped in a blanket, Anna yawns. **"Do svidaniya, spokoynoy nochi,"** she says.

Do svidaniya, spokoynoy nochi (До свидания, спокойной ночи)
→ duh svee-dah-nee-ya, spa-koy-noy noh-chee

Japan

Watashitachi wa Nihongo o hanashimasu
私たちは日本語を話します
We speak Japanese

Ohayō gozaimasu

"Ohayō gozaimasu!" says Yuki as we travel across Japan to see snowy Mount Fuji, the temples in Kyoto, and cherry blossoms blooming in spring. We enjoy sushi and rice balls for lunch with cups of green tea. Then we see a Sumo wrestling match.

Ohayō gozaimasu (おはようございます)
→ oh-hah-yoh go-zai-mass

We arrive in Tokyo, the biggest city in the world! We learn about Japanese samurai, tea ceremonies, and all the technology Japan is famous for. We visit the Tokyo Tower, Shibuya Crossing, and more.

For dinner, we slurp ramen noodles and watch bright signs flash in the busy streets. We say goodbye as the lanterns glow. **"Sayōnara, oyasumi,"** says Haru.

sayōnara, oyasumi (さようなら、おやすみ) → sah-yoh-nah-rah, oh-yah-soo-mee

China

Wǒmen shuō Zhōngwén
我们说中文
We speak Mandarin

"**Nǐ hǎo, zǎo ān,**" says Mei as we arrive in Beijing, the capital of China. In parks decorated with red lanterns, people practice gentle morning tai chi, moving in slow motion to focus and feel calm for the day ahead. We eat steamed dumplings and visit the Great Wall, which is so long you can see it from space!
We travel by high-speed train to Xi'an and are amazed by the 8,000 clay Terracotta Army soldiers.

Nǐ hǎo, zǎo ān (你好, 早安) → nee how, dzaow an

We see giant pandas munching on bamboo in Sichuan, the rivers of Guilin, and the busy skyline of Shanghai. We return to Beijing to finish our tour of China at the Forbidden City.

Dinner is a feast of noodles, rice, and crispy duck. As the moon rises over the lanterns, fireworks fill the sky. Li says, **"Zàijiàn, wǎn'ān,"** and we wave goodbye as we continue our journey.

Zàijiàn, wǎn'ān (再见，晚安) → dzai-jyen, wan-an

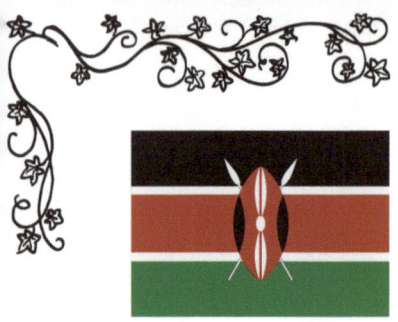

Kenya
Tunasema Kiswahili
We speak Swahili

"Jambo, asubuhi njema"

We travel across the Maasai Mara in Kenya. We spot elephants walking slowly through the tall golden grass, and lions sleeping under acacia trees. In the distance, Mount Kenya rises high with snow on its peak, watching over the land.
The air smells like earth and sunshine, and everything feels peaceful and wild. **"Jambo! asubuhi njema"** says Nia, waving as we begin our safari adventure.

Jambo! asubuhi njema → jahm-boh! ah-soo-boo-hee njeh-mah

In Nairobi, the capital of Kenya, we explore the busy markets and taste sweet mangoes and chapati. We visit the Giraffe Centre, where we feed giraffes from a tall platform, and then take a walk through Nairobi National Park to see zebras and rhinos just outside the city.

As the sun sets, we ride through the glowing streets and watch the city lights sparkle. We enjoy one last evening with music and dancing.
"Kwaheri, usiku mwema," says Amani as we wave goodbye.

Kwaheri, usiku mwema → kwah-heh-ree, oo-see-koo mweh-mah

Egypt

Natakallam al-'arabiyya
نتكلم العربية
We speak Arabic

"**Marḥaban, sabah el-kheir,**" says Layla as we arrive in Cairo, the capital of Egypt. We ride a camel near the Great Pyramids of Giza and see the Sphinx smiling in the sand. We sail on a boat called a felucca along the Nile River and snack on dates and figs.

Marḥaban, ṣabāḥ el-kheir سلامة، تصبح على خير.
→ Mar-ha-ban, sa-bah el-khair

We scuba dive on the coral reefs in the Red Sea. Eventually, we travel to Luxor to visit ancient temples, then explore quiet villages along the desert, stopping at colourful markets to smell the perfume oils and spices.

For dinner, we eat koshari and have molokhia soup. We watch a lively belly-dancing show, with colourful scarves twirling and drums beating. Lanterns flicker around the restaurant, casting dancing shadows on the walls. As stars twinkle over the palm trees, Amir says, **"Salāma, tisbah ʿala khayr."**

Salāma, tisbah ʿala khayr سلامة، تصبح على خير.
→ sa-la-mah toos-beeh ah-la khair

India

Hum Hindi bolte hain
हम हिंदी बोलते हैं
We speak Hindi

"Namaste, shubh prabhāt," says Anaya as we arrive at the Taj Mahal in Agra, where its white marble shines in the sun. In Jaipur, the Pink City, we ride elephants past royal palaces. We drink a warm cup of chai, then head to the busy streets to see Holi — the Festival of Colours, where everyone throws bright colour powder over each other.

Namaste, shubh prabhāt (नमस्ते, शुभ प्रभात)
→ nah-mah-stay, shoobh prah-bhaat

We travel to the capital city of New Delhi and learn about Diwali — the Festival of Lights. We take a tuktuk ride through the noisy, busy streets, looking at the people dressed in sarees, turbans, and kurtas.

We drink a mango lassi to keep cool in the heat and eat butter chicken, naan bread, and sweet gulab jamun for dessert.

As lanterns glow and fireflies dance, Aarav waves. **"Alvida, Śubh rātri,"** he says.

Alvida, Śubh rātri (अलविदा, शुभ रात्रि) → al-vee-dah, shoobh rah-tree

Brazil

Nós falamos português

We speak Portuguese

"Olá, Bom dia!" says Lucas as we arrive in Brazil. We visit the towering Christ the Redeemer statue, standing high above Rio de Janeiro with arms open wide. Down below, we walk along the colourful steps of Escadaria Selarón and listen to lively music in the streets.

We journey to the Amazon Rainforest, where bright parrots swoop overhead and monkeys swing from the trees. At the market, we taste juicy papaya and sweet brigadeiros, and watch street performers dance and drum with big smiles.

Olá, bom dia → oh-lah, boh-n jee-ah

We go to see a football (soccer) match—Brazil's favourite sport. Five-time world cup winners, they've won more than any other country! We stroll along Copacabana Beach, where the waves shimmer under the moon. Deep in the rainforest, night creatures wake up.

For dinner, we try feijoada stew and sweet grilled pineapple. We finish the evening watching people dance to samba rhythms, our feet tapping along.
We fall asleep to the sound of frogs and crickets.
"Tchau, boa noite," says Sofia.

Tchau, boa noite → chow, boh-ah noy-chee

Mexico

Hablamos español

We speak Spanish

In the warm sunshine of Mexico, we go on an adventure to Chichen Itza, the 3,000 year old ancient Mayan pyramid standing tall and proud. **"¡Hola, buenos días!"** says Juan.

We travel to the beaches of Cancún, the jungles of Chiapas, and the floating gardens of Xochimilco. We enjoy a tasty snack of churros dusted with cinnamon sugar. A lively mariachi band, dressed in traditional charro costumes, plays cheerful tunes on guitars and trumpets, while people clap and dance along.

Hola, buenos días → oh-lah, bweh-nos dee-ahs

We go for a swim in crystal-blue sinkholes called 'cenotes' before traveling to the capital, Mexico City.
We go to see lucha libre — a wrestling match with bright costumes and acrobatics. The crowd cheers loudly as the masked wrestlers leap, flip, and spin across the ring.

At night, we see a special festival, Día de los Muertos (Day of the Dead), where people dress up as skeletons and paint their faces to honour deceased loved ones, and connect with their ancestors.
We eat tacos, burritos, and enchiladas for dinner. We leave Mexico with full, happy bellies. **"Adiós, buenas noches,"** says Diego.

Our journey has come to an end. We head back home, wondering where our next adventure will take us!

Adiós, buenas noches → ah-dee-ohs, bweh-nas noh-ches

www.ingramcontent.com/pod-product-compliance
Lightning Source LLC
Chambersburg PA
CBHW041107070526
44583CB00002B/90